I

DECREE

FIRE

TO CONSUME AND

DESTROY WITHCHCRAFT POWERS

By Tella Olayeri

08023583168

Published By:

GOD'S LINK VENTURES

Email <u>tellaolayeri@gmail.com</u>

Website <u>http://tellaolayeri.com</u>

US Contact
Ruth Jack
14 Milewood Road
Verbank
N.Y.12585
U.S.A. +19176428989

APPRECIATION

I give special appreciation to my wife MRS NGOZI OLAYERI for her assistance in ensuring that this book is published and our children that played around us to encourage us day and night.

Also, this manuscript wouldn't have seen the light of the day, if not for the spiritual encouragement I gathered from my father in the Lord, Dr. D.K. OLUKOYA who served as spiritual mirror that brightens my hope to explore my calling (Evangelism).
We shall all reap our blessings in heaven but the battle to make heaven is not over, until it is won.

PREFACE

It is time you count gain not loss. There is power in prayer. You must learn how to decree against powers of darkness that trouble life and sink destiny. This book is specifically written to train your hands to war and your fingers for battle. Battles are fought and won. You must participate before you can be declared a winner.

This book is written to spiritually energize you to action in the battle of life. Put effort in what you do to count gain. Everyone born of flesh goes through one battle or the other. The Lord is there for you as a shield against principalities and powers and to ensure you are victorious in battles. Today, anointing of victory awaits you; the battle of life will not consume you.

Prayer is not magic, prayer is communicating with God to receive answer. Father Abraham prayed and received answer; Jacob prayed and received answer, David prayed prayers of Psalms and received answer. Elijah prayed fire prayer and received answer. Jesus Christ prayed and fasted before he went into his ministry.

This means there is power or powers that need to be addressed if you should excel in life. This book is written to address issues of life. The battle of life that must be crushed; opposition to breakthrough that must be alienated or else stagnancy and demotion will have better part of one's life. Failure have no friends, breakthrough does. You must strive to make it in life and defeat failure. All these can be achieved if you are in good health.

This book addressed it all. It will enable you to clear hurdles of life and be a champion. The book is loaded with spiritual vomited prayers that open heavens for your sake. You must not fold your arms if you want to succeed in life. You must apply right weapon to destroy works of darkness, and ensure you occupy mountain top. You are created to be a leader not a servant, the head and not the tail.

With prayer in this book no power shall sink your destiny. No evil arrow fired against you shall prosper. Pestilence that stalks in darkness shall fail in your life. The bottom line is, you are too loaded to be reduced to nothing. The Lord shall mightily stand by you as you count spoils after the prayer in this book.

Arise as a soldier of Christ; go to battle in prayer with this book. No barrier will hold you back. The Lord is your strength. Pick a copy.

GOOD NEWS!!!

My audiobook is now available, to get one visit acx.com and search **"Tella Olayeri."**

Brethren, to be loaded and reloaded visit: *amazon.com/author/tellaolayeri* for a full spiritual sojourn for my books.

Thanks.

PREVIOUS PUBLICATIONS OF THE AUTHOR

1. <u>100% CONFESSIONS and PROPHECIES to Locate Helpers and helpers to locate you</u>
2. <u>1000 Prayer Points for Children Breakthrough</u>
3. <u>1010 (One Thousand and Ten) DREAMS and Interpretations</u>
4. <u>2000 Dangerous Prayer for First Born</u>
5. <u>365 DREAMS and INTERPRETATIONS</u>
6. <u>430 Prayers to Cancel Bad Dreams and Overcome Witchcraft Powers part one (DREAMS AND YOU Book 1)</u>
7. <u>430 Prayers to Claim Good Dreams and Overcome Witchcraft Powers part two (DREAMS AND YOU Book 2)</u>
8. <u>630 Acidic Prayers: With Missile Prayer for Speedy Breakthrough, Healing and Deliverance</u>
9. <u>650 DREAMS AND INTERPRETATIONS</u>
10. <u>700 Prayers to Clear Unemployment Out of Your Way</u>
11. <u>720 Missile Prayers that Silence Enemies: Prayers that Bring Peace and Rest</u>
12. <u>740 Rocket Prayers that Break Satanic Embargo</u>
13. <u>777 Deliverance Prayers for Healing and Breakthrough</u>
14. <u>800 Deliverance Prayer for Middle Born: Daily Devotional for Teen and Adult</u>

40. <u>**Deliverance Prayer For Last Born: Daily Devotional for Teen and Adult**</u>

41. <u>**Deliverance Prayer for Middle Born: Daily Devotional for Teen and Adult**</u>

42. <u>**Deliverance Prayers for First Born: Daily Devotional for Teen and Adult**</u>

43. <u>**Dictionary of Dreams: The Dream Interpretation Dictionary With Symbols, Signs, and Meanings**</u>

44. <u>**Double Fire Double Thunder Prayer Book**</u>

45. <u>**Dreams and Visions and ways to Understand their Mysterious Meanings part one: The Dream Interpretation Dictionary Containing Symbols, Signs, and Meanings (DREAMS INTERPRETATION Book 1)**</u>

46. <u>**Dreams and Visions and ways to Understand their Mysterious Meanings part three: With Dreams Containing Symbols, Signs, Colors, Numbers and Meanings (DREAMS INTERPRETATION Book 3)**</u>

47. <u>**Dreams and Visions and ways to Understand their Mysterious Meanings part two: The Dream Interpretation Dictionary Containing Symbols, Signs, and Meanings (DREAMS INTERPRETATION Book 2)**</u>

48. <u>**Enough of Sudden Diseases and Infirmities: With Biblical Secrets to Divine Healing against Strange Sickness, Pains, Diseases and Infirmities**</u>

49. <u>**Fire for Fire part one: (PRAYER BOOK Book 1)**</u>

See all at: **amazon.com/author/tellaolayeri**

Table of Contents

CHAPTER 1

THE BATTLE OF LIFE SHALL NOT CONSUME ME

Psalm 33:18-22

18. *But the eyes of the LORD are on those who fear him, on those whose hope is in his unfailing love,*

19. To deliver them from death and keep them alive in famine.

20. We wait in hope for the LORD; he is our help and our shield.

21. In him our hearts rejoice, for we trust in his holy name.

22. May your unfailing love be with us, LORD, even as we put our hope in you.

2 Peter 2:13-15

13. They will be paid back with harm for the harm they have done. Their idea of pleasure is to carouse in broad daylight. They are blots and blemishes, reveling in their pleasures while they feast with you.

14. With eyes full of adultery, they never stop sinning; they seduce the unstable; they are experts in greed an accursed brood!

15. They have left the straight way and wandered off to follow the way of Balaam son of Beor, who loved the wages of wickedness.

Psalm 91:5-7

5. You will not fear the terror of night, nor the arrow that flies by day,

6. Nor the pestilence that stalks in the darkness, nor the plague that destroys at midday.

7. A thousand may fall at your side, ten thousand at your right hand, but it will not come near you.

PRAYER POINTS

1. I thank God, for lifting me up when I fall, in the name of Jesus.
2. I thank God, for making me more than a conqueror in the battle of life.
3. I thank you O Lord, for your support and love for me, in the name of Jesus.

4. I thank my God, for his faithfulness to my family, friends, and neighbours, in the name of Jesus.

5. I praise my God, the prayer answering God, in the name of Jesus

6. I thank my God, all seeing, all knowing, all powerful God, in the name of Jesus.

7. O Lord, forgive me in the area I have been lazy in prayer.

8. Lord Jesus, have mercy upon me in the day of trouble.

9. Lord Jesus forgive me, so that I may overcome the battles of my life.

10. Lord Jesus forgive me, so that my eyes can spiritually open to what happens in my life.

11. O Lord, lay your hands of forgiveness upon my life, in the name of Jesus.

12. Lord Jesus, forgive me as I forgive others that offend me, in the name of Jesus.

13. I cover myself with blood of Jesus against battle of life in the name of Jesus.

14. I cover myself with blood of Jesus, to defend me when battle arises in the name of Jesus.

15. Blood of Jesus, speak for me in the day of trouble in the name of Jesus.

16. I drink blood of Jesus, to purge every satanic deposit in my life in the name of Jesus.

17. I drink blood of Jesus, to improve my righteousness in the name of Jesus.
18. Blood of Jesus, strengthen me in the midst of odd situation in the name of Jesus.
19. Holy Ghost Power, see me through in this prayer in the name of Jesus.
20. Holy Spirit Divine, speak for me where I am weak in the name of Jesus.
21. Holy Spirit, lay hand of victory upon me, to endure and win battles of life in the name of Jesus.
22. Holy Spirit, let your glorious light shine upon me in the name of Jesus.
23. Holy Spirit, energise me in the area of laziness in prayer in the name of Jesus.
24. Holy Spirit, deposit spirit of perfect holiness in me, that battle of life shall not pollute in the name of Jesus.
25. O Lord save me from self created problem, in the name of Jesus.
26. Lord Jesus, be the fighter and conqueror of the battles of my life, in the name of Jesus.
27. Every battle that rises at night to sink my destiny, scatter, in the name of Jesus.
28. Every arrow that flies by day, be silenced, in the name of Jesus.

29. Every evil arrow fired against my destiny, backfire, in the name of Jesus.
30. Every pestilence that stalks in darkness to destroy me, expire in the name of Jesus.
31. Every plague assign to consume me, expire, in the name of Jesus.
32. Every battle that surrounds me scatter, in the name of Jesus.
33. Every evil eye monitoring me for evil, go blind in the name of Jesus.
34. Every terror of the night organized to turn my life upside down, scatter, in the name of Jesus.
35. Every fear from pit of hell against my life, scatter, in the name of Jesus.
36. Powers that hide in the dark to kill me, die in my place, in the name of Jesus.
37. Every plague from pit of hell, expire in the name of Jesus.
38. O Lord, pay my enemy back with evil they plan for me, in the name of Jesus.
39. Every plan of darkness against my life to cause sorrow in my life, scatter, in the name of Jesus.
40. Broad day light attack against my destiny, backfire and scatter, in the name of Jesus.
41. Deceivers around me be put to shame, in the name of Jesus.

42. Evil attachment in my eyes that makes me sin, expire, in the name of Jesus.

43. Spirit of lust in my life, come out and expire, in the name of Jesus.

44. Powers that love wages of wickedness, expire with it, in the name of Jesus.

45. O Lord, rebuke and silence my enemy in the name of Jesus.

46. Wicked prophecy against my destiny backfire, in the name of Jesus.

47. O Lord arise, support my cause for breakthrough, in the name of Jesus.

48. O Lord, deliver me from grip of death, in the name of Jesus.

49. I shall lie above famine and disaster, in the name of Jesus.

50. O Lord, crown my hope with breakthrough, in the name of Jesus.

51. The Lord is my shield, I fear no foe, in the name of Jesus.

52. Heavenly honey of joy, fill my heart, in the name of Jesus.

53. Unfailing love of God, come upon me, in the name of Jesus.

54. I shall not tarry in the wilderness of confusion, in the name of Jesus.

55. O Lord, let your glory cover me round about, in the name of Jesus.

56. Lord Jesus, let me know who I am to you, so that I can amend in my fallen areas, in the name of Jesus.

57. Lord Jesus, make me container fire brand that scatter works of darkness, in the name of Jesus.

58. Lord Jesus, be the lifter of my head against every battle in the name of Jesus.

59. O Lord, deliver me from the sword of the wicked, in the name of Jesus.

60. O Lord, let songs of deliverance bust out of my mouth, in the name of Jesus.

61. O Lord, silence powers that lie in wait for my blood, in the name of Jesus.

62. Lord Jesus, do great and mighty things in my life, in the name of Jesus.

63. Guardian angels of God keep watch over me 24 hours every day, in the name of Jesus.

64. Every hidden arrow fired against me from my place of birth, backfire and kill your sender.

65. Witchcraft record that contain my life for elimination, catch fire and roast to ashes, in the name of Jesus.

66. Every power of the sand aimed to paralyze and scatter my destiny, backfire against powers behind it in the name of Jesus.

67. Powers that are against me at the door of breakthrough die, in the name of Jesus.
68. Every battle of life assigned to consume me and my household, scatter in the name of Jesus.
69. O God arise, let the battle of the wicked consume them, in the name of Jesus.
70. Powers assign to reduce me to nothing, die, in the name of Jesus.
71. O Lord, let your glory shine upon me, in the name of Jesus.
72. Bulldozer of God come to my defense, crush enemy of my soul, grind them to nothing, in the name of Jesus.
73. Witchcraft blood in my blood line, flowing against my survival, dry up, in the name of Jesus.
74. Powers that pursue my parents to destroy them, and now after my life, expire, in the name of Jesus.
75. The mistakes and omission of my parents shall not be added to the battle I face in life, in the name of Jesus.
76. Every plan of the enemy to turn my life upside down, scatter, in the name of Jesus.
77. Satanic odour in my body, pushing helpers away, expire, in the name of Jesus.

78. Every labour as a result of curse pronounced against me, be broken in the name of Jesus.

CHAPTER 2

I CRUSH OPPOSITION OF MY RISING

Isaiah 43:1-2

1. But now, this is what the LORD says he who created you, Jacob, he who formed you, Israel: "Do not fear, for I have redeemed you; I have summoned you by name; you are mine.

2. When you pass through the waters, I will be with you; and when you pass through the rivers, they will not sweep over you. When you walk through the fire, you will not be burned; the flames will not set you ablaze.

Psalm 35:1-6

5. May they be like chaff before the wind, with the angel of the LORD driving them away;

6. May their path be dark and slippery, with the angel of the LORD pursuing them.

1 Peter 5:6-9

6. Humble yourselves, therefore, under God's mighty hand, that he may lift you up in due time.

7. Cast all your anxiety on him because he cares for you.

8. Be alert and of sober mind. Your enemy the devil prowls around like a roaring lion looking for someone to devour.

9. Resist him, standing firm in the faith, because you know that the family of believers throughout the world is undergoing the same kind of sufferings.

PRAYER POINTS

1. I thank you O Lord, for the salvation of my soul in the name of Jesus.
2. I thank you O Lord, for the baptism of my soul and my family with spirit of Holy Ghost in the name of Jesus.
3. I thank you O Lord, for your protection upon my life in the name of Jesus.
4. I thank you O Lord, for your provision and health care in the name of Jesus.
5. I thank you O Lord, for crushing opposition that rise up against me in the name of Jesus.
6. I thank you O Lord, enemy shall not dictate to me in the name of Jesus.
7. Holy Spirit, arise be the attacker of my enemy in the name of Jesus.
8. O Lord, forgive me of sins that bring disunity in my family in the name of Jesus.

9. O Lord, forgive me of known and unknown sins that makes you look elsewhere.
10. O Lord, forgive me sins that make my adversaries laugh at me in the name of Jesus.
11. O Lord, forgive me sins that brought no peace to life in the name of Jesus.
12. O Lord forgive me sins that make me prayerless in the name of Jesus.
13. I cover myself with blood of Jesus, to silence every opposition to my rising in the name of Jesus.
14. I drink blood of Jesus, to energize me against opposition in the name of Jesus.
15. I spray blood of Jesus, on the face of opposition that vow I shall not make it in life in the name of Jesus.
16. Blood of Jesus, be a barricade between me and powers of darkness in the name of Jesus.
17. Blood of Jesus, flow around me and do great exploit in the name of Jesus.
18. Blood of Jesus, nullify adversaries of the enemy against me in the name of Jesus.
19. Holy Spirit arise fight my battle till I win, in the name of Jesus.
20. Holy Spirit, come upon me mightily in the name of Jesus.

21. Holy Spirit, let your spirit work in me in the name of Jesus.
22. Holy Spirit, intervene in my life for great exploit in the name of Jesus.
23. Holy Spirit, draw me to prayer room of God, in the name of Jesus.
24. Holy Spirit, make me your child, feed me with heavenly spirit, in the name of Jesus.
25. O Lord, declare your glory upon me, in the name of Jesus.
26. O Lord, let fire of revival fall upon and crush powers opposing work of God, in the name of Jesus.
27. O Lord my redeemer, crush every opposition of my destiny, in the name of Jesus.
28. My name shall not succumb to Satan in the name of Jesus.
29. Any power summoning my name for evil, die, in the name of Jesus.
30. When I pass through the waters the Lord shall be with me, in the name of Jesus.
31. When I pass through the rivers they will not sweep over me, in the name of Jesus.
32. When I walk through the fire, it will not burn me, in the name of Jesus.
33. When I walk through the fire, the flames will not set me ablaze, in the name of Jesus.

34. I receive angelic visitation and support in what I do, in the name of Jesus.

35. Today, I am a candidate of signs and wonders, in the name of Jesus.

36. I receive anointing of victory, in the name of Jesus.

37. Every agent of darkness assign to destroy me, die, in the name of Jesus.

38. I revoke every satanic opposition against my destiny, in the name of Jesus.

39. O Lord, contend with those who contend with me, in the name of Jesus.

40. O Lord, fight against those who fight against me, in the name of Jesus.

41. Angel of God, brandish spear and javelin against my enemy in the name of Jesus.

42. O Lord, take shield and buckler to support me, in the name of Jesus.

43. Every stubborn pursuer that rise against me, summersault and die, in the name of Jesus.

44. Those who seek my life be exposed and be disgraced, in the name of Jesus.

45. Those who plan to ruin my destiny, gather together for destruction in the name of Jesus.

46. Those that plan evil against me, be turned to chaff and swept away by the wind, in the name of Jesus.

47. Thou enemy of my soul, may your way be dark and slippery, in the name of Jesus.
48. O Lord, crown me and lift me up, in the presence of my enemy, in the name of Jesus.
49. O Lord, I cast all my anxiety on you, you are my saviour, in the name of Jesus.
50. Every dark lion prowling about in order to consume me die, in the name of Jesus.
51. I resist the devil and it shall be well with me, in the name of Jesus.
52. O Lord, empower me to crush serpents and scorpions that come my way in the name of Jesus.
53. O Lord, declare upon me, no weapon fashioned against me shall prosper in the name of Jesus.
54. O Lord, deliver me from the wicked, do not let me be ashamed, in the name of Jesus.
55. Lord Jesus, enlarge my coast against every opposition in the name of Jesus.
56. Lord Jesus, redeem me from every curse of opposition in the name of Jesus.
57. O Lord, turn me to your power house that cannot be insulted by opposition, in the name of Jesus.
58. Lord Jesus, let your power reside in me, in the name of Jesus.

59. O Lord, silence every hindering forces against my prosperity, in the name of Jesus.
60. Lord Jesus, let riches and honour be my portion.
61. The Lord is my shepherd, opposition power shall not take over my destiny, in the name of Jesus.
62. O heavens open, let my glory shine, in the name of Jesus.
63. Chains of darkness in my hands break in the name of Jesus.
64. Chain of darkness in my leg, break in the name of Jesus.
65. O Lord, reverse former financial crisis to wealth in the name of Jesus.
66. O Lord, silence every business competitor that is against me in the spirit in the name of Jesus.
67. O Lord, open my destiny to sources of wealth in the name of Jesus.
68. I bind and render useless every opposition forces against my life, in the name of Jesus.
69. O Lord, help me, let the prophecy of the enemy work against them, in the name of Jesus.
70. Witchdoctor that raise evil altar against me, be exposed and be disgraced, in the name of Jesus.
71. I unplug my destiny from power of darkness in the name of Jesus.

72. My case files in the coven of darkness, catch fire and roast to ashes, in the name of Jesus.
73. Every evil bewitchment organized for my sake, scatter, in the name of Jesus.
74. Those who dwell in darkness be consumed by darkness, in the name of Jesus.
75. O Lord, let the feet of the enemy fall into the net design for me, in the name of Jesus.

CHAPTER 3

THE GOLIATH AND STONGMAN AFTER MY STAR SHALL FAIL

Psalm 3:6-8

6. *I will not fear though tens of thousands assail me on every side.*

7. *Arise, LORD! Deliver me, my God! Strike all my enemies on the jaw; break the teeth of the wicked.*

8. *From the LORD comes deliverance. May your blessing be on your people.*

Ephesians 6:11-13

11. *Put on the full armor of God, so that you can take your stand against the devil's schemes.*

12. *For our struggle is not against flesh and blood, but against the rulers, against the authorities, against the powers of this dark world and against the spiritual forces of evil in the heavenly realms.*

13. *Therefore put on the full armor of God, so that when the day of evil comes, you may be able to stand your ground, and after you have done everything, to stand.*

Isaiah 54:14-17

14. In righteousness you will be established: Tyranny will be far from you; you will have nothing to fear. Terror will be far removed; it will not come near you.

15. If anyone does attack you, it will not be my doing; whoever attacks you will surrender to you.

16. "See, it is I who created the blacksmith who fans the coals into flame and forges a weapon fit for its work. And it is I who have created the destroyer to wreak havoc;

17. No weapon forged against you will prevail, and you will refute every tongue that accuses you. This is the heritage of the servants of the LORD, and this is their vindication from me," declares the LORD.

PRAYER POINTS

1. I thank you O Lord, for your protection upon my life in the name of Jesus.
2. I praise the Lord, who shall silence the strongman in the corridor of my life in the name of Jesus.
3. I thank God for his mercy endureth forever in the name of Jesus.

4. I thank God, who put smiles to my face in the name of Jesus.
5. I thank God, who defeats the enemy even before the battle begins in the name of Jesus.
6. I thank God, for removing fear from my heart in the name of Jesus.
7. Lord Jesus, have mercy upon me and my household in the name of Jesus.
8. O Lord, by your mercy upon me, silence every Goliath troubling my life in the name of Jesus.
9. Lord Jesus, let me experience your forgiveness 24 hours every day in the name of Jesus.
10. The mercy of God upon me shall drive strongman away from me in the name of Jesus.
11. By your mercy Lord, pull me out of captivity, in the name of Jesus.
12. I plead for mercy and forgiveness, in the name of Jesus.
13. I drink blood of Jesus, to give me power to face every Goliath assign against my life in the name of Jesus.
14. Blood of Jesus, protect my star, in the name of Jesus.
15. Blood of Jesus, paralyze, hands of the wicked targeting my star in the name of Jesus.
16. I cover myself with blood of Jesus against attacks of darkness in the name of Jesus.

17. Blood of Jesus, be a barricade between me and powers of darkness in the name of Jesus.

18. Blood of Jesus, blindfold Satan and his agents running after my life in the name of Jesus.

19. Holy Spirit Divine, fight every strongman assign against my destiny in the name of Jesus.

20. Holy Spirit, lay hand of strength upon me, in the name of Jesus.

21. Holy Spirit, see to my situation, help me out, in the name of Jesus.

22. Holy Spirit, guide my steps to breakthrough, in the name of Jesus.

23. Holy Spirit, plant seed of wisdom in my life, that will silence strongman of my life in the name of Jesus.

24. Holy Spirit, plant seed of joy in my life, in the name of Jesus.

25. O Lord, silence every strongman of my father's house that vow I will not make it in life in the name of Jesus.

26. O Lord, silence every strongman of my mother's house that vow to naked me, in the name of Jesus.

27. Tyranny of darkness against my life, expire, in the name of Jesus.

28. Dark altar giving support to my enemy, catch fire and roast to ashes, in the name of Jesus.

29. Arrow of terror fired against me, backfire, in the name of Jesus.

30. Every attack against my destiny, scatter in the name of Jesus.

31. O Lord, let those who attack me surrender, in the name of Jesus.

32. Powers of darkness against me, sink in the name of Jesus.

33. No weapon fashioned by Goliath of darkness against me shall prosper, in the name of Jesus.

34. Every tongue that accuse me wrongly, be put to shame in the name of Jesus.

35. Enemy shall not take over my inheritance in the name of Jesus.

36. Thou power of God, move me forward by fire, in the name of Jesus.

37. Any power planning demotion and failure for me, expire in the name of Jesus.

38. Every Goliath harassing me in the spirit, die in the name of Jesus.

39. Goliath assign to cause fear in my life, die in the name of Jesus.

40. I will not fear tens of thousands drawn up against me in the name of Jesus.

41. O Lord, deliver me of strongman that rise up against me, in the name of Jesus.

42. O Lord break the teeth of the wicked that vow to consume me, in the name of Jesus.

43. O Lord, deliver me from the wickedness of the wicked in the name of Jesus.

44. Every enemy that surround me in order to pull me down and disgrace me, die in the name of Jesus.

45. O Lord, disgrace enemy that take pleasure in evil against my household, in the name of Jesus.

46. O Lord, deliver me from the hands of bloodthirsty and deceitful men, in the name of Jesus.

47. O Lord, dress me in your full armour against the evil in the name of Jesus.

48. Every ruler of darkness that rise up against me, scatter, in the name of Jesus.

49. When the day of evil come, my God shall empower me to defeat them in the name of Jesus.

50. O Lord, extinguish all the flaming arrow of the wicked, in the name of Jesus.

51. Every unholy war against me scatter in the name of Jesus.

52. O Lord, silence every strongman of my In-law's house that vow to pull me down, in the name of Jesus.

53. O Lord, break every covenant made on my behalf with any strongman molesting me in the name of Jesus.

54. Every strongman behind my problem die in the name of Jesus.

55. Thunder of God, uproot evil tree that turn to strongman in my father's house, in the name of Jesus.

56. Plantation of darkness causing problem for my star, die to your root, in the name of Jesus.

57. Evil handwriting against my star, be nullified in the name of Jesus.

58. Every darkness assign to swallow my star, clear away in the name of Jesus.

59. Powers assign to put my star in bondage, expire in the name of Jesus.

60. I break all curses pronounced by strongman against my destiny, in the name of Jesus.

61. O Lord, silence every Goliath of my father's house assign to pull me down at the edge of breakthrough in the name of Jesus.

62. Star hunters targeting the star of my life, for evil, die in the name of Jesus.

63. Powers that gang up against my star, die, in the name of Jesus.

64. My star, arise and shine, in the name of Jesus.

65. O Lord, let every violence assign to consume me, scatter in the name of Jesus.
66. O Lord, dismantle barricades of strongman targeted against me in the name of Jesus.
67. Every strongman behind the problem confronting me in life, die in the name of Jesus.
68. Lord Jesus, make my heart glad, let my inmost rejoice to your glory in the name of Jesus.
69. Strangers guiding the door of my destiny, die in the name of Jesus.
70. Thou evil door built by strangers to imprison me, I pull you down, in the name of Jesus.
71. I bind every Goliath that troubles my soul, in the name of Jesus.
72. Goliath of impossibility, hunting my destiny in order to destroy it, die in the name of Jesus.
73. Anywhere my name is mentioned for evil, blood of Jesus appear and silence them in the name of Jesus.
74. Every strongman or woman denying me my freedom, enough is enough expire, in the name of Jesus.
75. Every enemy of my progress, meet double failure in the name of Jesus.

CHAPTER 4

I SPEAK AGAINST FAILURE

Zephaniah 1:13

13. Their wealth will be plundered, their houses demolished. Though they build houses, they will not live in them; though they plant vineyards, they will not drink the wine. "

Isaiah 22:21-24

21. I will clothe him with your robe and fasten your sash around him and hand your authority over to him. He will be a father to those who live in Jerusalem and to the people of Judah.

22. I will place on his shoulder the key to the house of David; what he opens no one can shut, and what he shuts no one can open.

23. I will drive him like a peg into a firm place; he will become a seat of honor for the house of his father.

24. All the glory of his family will hang on him: its offspring and offshoots all its lesser vessels, from the bowls to all the jars.

Psalm 34:6-10

6. This poor man called, and the LORD heard him; he saved him out of all his troubles.

7. The angel of the LORD encamps around those who fear him, and he delivers them.

8. Taste and see that the LORD is good; blessed is the one who takes refuge in him.

9. Fear the LORD, you his holy people, for those who fear him lack nothing.

10. The lions may grow weak and hungry, but those who seek the LORD lack no good thing.

PRAYER POINTS

1. I thank my God, who protects me against powers of darkness in the name of Jesus.
2. I thank you Lord for protecting my interest against failure in the name of Jesus.
3. I thank you Lord for the blessing and success that awaits me in the name of Jesus.
4. I thank you Lord for supplying all my needs according to your riches and glory in the name of Jesus.
5. I thank my God who will open heavens for my sake in the name of Jesus.
6. I thank you Lord for the joy that awaits me in the name of Jesus.

7. Lord Jesus, lay hands of mercy and glory upon my life in the name of Jesus.
8. Lord Jesus, I repent of my sins forgive me by your power in the name of Jesus.
9. Lord Jesus, forgive me of destructive habits keeping me backward in the name of Jesus.
10. Lord Jesus, forgive me of sins causing problem in my life in the name of Jesus.
11. Lord Jesus, forgive me of sins that keep me in darkness in the name of Jesus.
12. Lord Jesus, by your mercy dismantle problems in my life in the name of Jesus.
13. Blood of Jesus, break every embargo that refuse to let me go in the name of Jesus.
14. I drink blood of Jesus, to strengthen me and give me edge over competitors in the name of Jesus.
15. I drink blood of Jesus, to dissolve and kill agents of darkness in my life in the name of Jesus.
16. Blood of Jesus, resurrect good thing that is dead in my life, in the name of Jesus.
17. I drink blood of Jesus, to purge and destroy evil deposit in my life in the name of Jesus.
18. Blood of Jesus, kill satanic seed in my life in the name of Jesus.

19. Holy Spirit, visit me afresh today, in the name of Jesus.

20. Holy Ghost Power, fight my battle for me, in the name of Jesus.

21. Holy Ghost, hold my hand, pull me out among dunghill and promote me, in the name of Jesus.

22. Holy Spirit arise, wage war against those who rise against me, in the name of Jesus.

23. I pluck my destiny to socket of Holy Ghost, in the name of Jesus.

24. Holy Spirit, speak to my life and let wonders happen today, in the name of Jesus.

25. Lord Jesus, invoke rain of abundance of blessing upon me, in the name of Jesus.

26. O Lord, let wealth and riches locate my life, in the name of Jesus.

27. Enemies that vow to plunder my wealth, die, in the name of Jesus.

28. My wealth in the warehouse of darkness, I recover you by fire, in the name of Jesus.

29. Dark powers ready to demolish my home, paralyze and die, in the name of Jesus.

30. Powers that vow to render me homeless and put me in shame die, in the name of Jesus.

31. Those that vow I will build but not live in them, shall fail in the name of Jesus.

32. Those that vow I will plant but not harvest shall fail in the name of Jesus.

33. Those that vow I will not laugh or dance over my sweat shall fail in the name of Jesus.

34. Powers counting days, weeks and year of maturity to attack me, die before maturity day, in the name of Jesus.

35. Glory killers in my father's house, shall meet double failure in the name of Jesus.

36. Let the day enemy plan to kill me be a day of trouble and ruin to them, in the name of Jesus.

37. I shall not live in distress and anguish, in the name of Jesus.

38. My household shall not live in darkness and gloom, in the name of Jesus.

39. Every fortified environment of the enemy, catch fire and burn down, in the name of Jesus.

40. Fierce anger of God, visit and destroy stubborn pursuers against me, in the name of Jesus.

41. Powers assign to turn my household to wasteland, die in the name of Jesus.

42. O Lord, clothe me with garment of authority and breakthrough in the name of Jesus.

43. O Lord, settle me in my Jerusalem, house of peace and prosperity in the name of Jesus.

44. O Lord, give me the key of David that opens no one can shut, in the name of Jesus.

45. O Lord, give me the key of David that shuts no one can open, in the name of Jesus.

46. O Lord, give me everlasting honour, enemy cannot contend with, in the name of Jesus.

47. O Lord, empower me, drive me like a peg into a firm place, that cannot be shaken or uprooted by the enemy, in the name of Jesus.

48. I recover every lost glory of my family, in the name of Jesus.

49. O Lord, save me out of all my troubles in the name of Jesus.

50. Angel of the living God encamp around me and defend me, in the name of Jesus.

51. Fear of God, envelope my heart, to hear from God and be blessed, in the name of Jesus.

52. The Lion may grow weak and hungry, I shall not lack in the name of Jesus.

53. O God arise, change my destiny for better, in the name of Jesus.

54. O Lord, program blessings to my life, in the name of Jesus.

55. Lord Jesus, speak to the works of my hand to multiply by fire, in the name of Jesus.

56. O Lord, give me strength to follow your plan for my life, in the name of Jesus.

57. O Lord, let arrow of failure fired against me, backfire to the sender, in the name of Jesus.

58. O Lord, fill my mouth with riddles of the wise, in the name of Jesus.

59. O Lord, let helpers pour out their heart to me to help me, in the name of Jesus.

60. O Lord, do not reject me when I call upon you, in the name of Jesus.

61. O Lord, accept me anytime I stretch hands unto you in prayer in the name of Jesus.

62. My soul, receive every rebuke of God so that I won't go into untimely grave in the name of Jesus.

63. O Lord, let the earth open and swallow my problem in the name of Jesus.

64. Holy Ghost, destroy evil dedication that put me in bondage, in the name of Jesus.

65. O Lord, destroy every bondage that captivate my parents and now targeting me for destruction in the name of Jesus.

66. O Lord, remove cup of failure in my family dining table, in the name of Jesus.

67. Thunder of God, uproot and destroy plantation of darkness in the garden of my life in the name of Jesus.

68. O Lord, let the legs of Mr. Failure advancing at me paralyze in the name of Jesus.

69. Satanic animal wondering about in my home in order to keep me in bondage, die, in the name of Jesus.
70. Demons targeting my destiny to be in bondage, die in the name of Jesus.
71. The thoughts of the wicked shall not prevail over me, in the name of Jesus.
72. My legs, receive heavenly power, march and kill spirit of poverty and lack troubling me, in the name of Jesus.
73. My destiny, be separated from failure in the name of Jesus.
74. Award of hardship and failure assign for me in the spirit, catch fire and roast to ashes, in the name of Jesus.
75. Every pain of financial failure keeping my soul down, expire, in the name of Jesus.
76. O Lord, let your light shine upon every darkness around me, and chase dark powers away in the name of Jesus.
77. Satanic sacrifice carried out to stagnate my life, backfire, in the name of Jesus.
78. Every seal fashion against my destiny, break in the name of Jesus.

CHAPTER 5

O LORD STRENGTHEN MY HEALTH

James 5:13-16

13. *Is anyone among you in trouble? Let them pray. Is anyone happy? Let them sing songs of praise.*

14. *Is anyone among you sick? Let them call the elders of the church to pray over them and anoint them with oil in the name of the Lord.*

15. *And the prayer offered in faith will make the sick person well; the Lord will raise them up. If they have sinned, they will be forgiven.*

16. *Therefore confess your sins to each other and pray for each other so that you may be healed. The prayer of a righteous person is powerful and effective.*

Jeremiah 30:16-17

16. *But all who devour you will be devoured; all your enemies will go into exile. Those who plunder you will be plundered; all who make spoil of you I will despoil.*

17. But I will restore you to health and heal your wounds,' declares the LORD, 'because you are called an outcast, Zion for whom no one cares.'

Isaiah 65:20-23

20. Never again will there be in it an infant who lives but a few days, or an old man who does not live out his years; the one who dies at a hundred will be thought a mere child; the one who fails to reach a hundred will be considered accursed.

21. They will build houses and dwell in them; they will plant vineyards and eat their fruit.

22. No longer will they build houses and others live in them, or plant and others eat. For as the days of a tree, so will be the days of my people; my chosen ones will long enjoy the work of their hands.

23. They will not labor in vain, nor will they bear children doomed to misfortune; for they will be a people blessed by the LORD, they and their descendants with them.

PRAYER POINTS

1. I thank my God, who protects me from ill-health of all kinds in the name of Jesus

2. Thank you Jesus for your protection upon me and my household in the name of Jesus

3. I thank you Lord for your healing upon my life in the name of Jesus

4. I thank my God who breaks yokes of darkness upon me in the name of Jesus

5. I thank my God who put smiles of bill of clean health in my face in the name of Jesus

6. I thank God for his love and mercy upon my household in the name of Jesus

7. O Lord, have mercy upon me, make me great in your kingdom in the name of Jesus

8. O Lord have mercy upon me so that my health can be normal in the name of Jesus

9. Lord Jesus, I need your mercy and forgiveness, let it be total in the name of Jesus

10. O Lord, don't look elsewhere, my sin drowns me, forgive me, in the name of Jesus

11. Lord Jesus, I plead for mercy and forgiveness, let it be, so that I can praise you more.

12. Lord Jesus, lay your hand of mercy and forgiveness upon me in the name of Jesus

13. Blood of Jesus, let ill-health symptoms leave my blood, in the name of Jesus.

14. I soak myself in the pool blood of Jesus, for total cleansing in the name of Jesus

15. I drink blood of Jesus, to purge me of impurities that may affect my health in the name of Jesus

16. I drink blood of Jesus, to kill evil deposits in my blood system in the name of Jesus

17. I plead blood of Jesus upon me, to serve as arrow proof against evil arrow in the name of Jesus

18. I break every covenant with ill-health, by the power in the blood of Jesus.

19. Holy Spirit let divine healing be my portion, in the name of Jesus.

20. Holy Spirit Divine, strengthen me beyond imagination of people in the name of Jesus

21. Holy Spirit, lay hands of miracle upon me, in the name of Jesus.

22. Holy Spirit, come upon me to silence every Goliath of bad health tormenting me.

23. Holy Spirit, give me discerning spirit to forge ahead in life in the name of Jesus

24. Holy Spirit, heal me, both flesh and blood, in the name of Jesus.

25. O Lord, speak woe to all powers assign to deaden my health, in the name of Jesus.

26. Lord Jesus, give me merry heart that do good like medicine of joy and healing in the name of Jesus

27. My years on earth shall not be shortened by sickness or disease in the name of Jesus.

28. Evil arrow fired against my health, backfire to your sender, in the name of Jesus.
29. Powers assign to devalue my health, I am not your candidate, quit my life and die, in the name of Jesus.
30. O Lord, let me live to old age and live out my years in good health, in the name of Jesus.
31. Every cause of untimely death pronounced against me, break in the name of Jesus.
32. I will build and occupy my house in good health in the name of Jesus.
33. I will plant and harvest in good health, in the name of Jesus.
34. I shall not build, and others will take over as spoil, in the name of Jesus.
35. I shall not plant, and others harvest the fruit of my labour, in the name of Jesus.
36. Powers assigned to attack me and cut my life short, die, in the name of Jesus.
37. I will long enjoy the works of my hands to the glory of God, in the name of Jesus.
38. I will not bear children doomed to misfortune or destruction, in the name of Jesus.
39. My lineage shall not know sorrow in the name of Jesus.
40. Satanic powers assign to devour me, be devoured, in the name of Jesus.

41. Bad health assign from pit of hell to devour me, expire, in the name of Jesus.
42. I fire arrow of God against my enemy and command them to exile forever, in the name of Jesus.
43. O Lord, heal my wounds in the name of Jesus.
44. I shall not be an outcast in the name of Jesus.
45. I shall not be a spoil in the camp of the enemy in the name of Jesus.
46. O Lord, build my health, save me from the hand of untimely death, in the name of Jesus.
47. Storm of darkness around my home, disappear in the name of Jesus.
48. I shall not weep over my health situation in the name of Jesus.
49. My health shall not be in trouble in the name of Jesus.
50. I will sing songs of praise to the Lord, that I am in good health and healthy in the name of Jesus.
51. O Lord, anoint me with oil of deliverance that brings good health in the name of Jesus.
52. O Lord, raise me up above bad health in the name of Jesus.
53. Every arrow of death fired against me, backfire to the sender in the name of Jesus.
54. Every power threatening my health, expire, in the name of Jesus.

55. Lord Jesus my Doctor, you are my Great Physician, heal me today in the name of Jesus

56. O Lord, keep my bones from rot in the name of Jesus.

57. Lord Jesus, by your power, redeem me from the power of the grave.

58. O Lord, let my bones operate in excellence, in the name of Jesus.

59. O Lord, let my flesh not decay or rotten while I am alive, in the name of Jesus.

60. O Lord, let my leg operate in excellence all the time, in the name of Jesus.

61. O Lord, let my eyes never go blind, in the name of Jesus.

62. O Lord, let my mouth operate in excellence in all situations in the name of Jesus.

63. Lord Jesus, answer me in this prayer, let my health improve by fire in the name of Jesus

64. O Lord, lay your hand of deliverance upon me today in the name of Jesus.

65. Every embargo upon my health, break in the name of Jesus.

66. I shall not trade my health with kingdom of darkness in the name of Jesus

67. Evil handwriting against my health be nullified with blood of Jesus.

68. Health bondage in my life, break, in the name of Jesus.

69. Every arrow of sickness fired against my life, backfire in the name of Jesus.

70. I walk out of captivity of sickness and disease in the name of Jesus.

71. O Lord, renew my youth like the eagle and let me grow in strength, in the name of Jesus.

72. Every weapon fashioned against my health, break to pieces, in the name of Jesus.

73. Every evil assign to befall me this year, scatter in the name of Jesus.

74. Every root of sickness in my life be uprooted, in the name of Jesus.

75. Every plantation of bad health in the garden of my life, be uprooted in the name of Jesus.

76. Every enchantment and divination against my health be nullified, in the name of Jesus.

77. Poison in my body when I was a child, be neutralized by blood of Jesus.

78. O Lord, let not your wrath, promote bad health in my body in the name of Jesus

YOU HAVE BATTLES TO WIN
TRY THESE BOOKS

1. <u>COMMAND THE DAY: DAILY PRAYER BOOK</u>

Each day of the week is loaded with meanings and divine assurance. God did not create each day of the week for the fun of it. Blessings, success, gifts, resources, hopes, portfolios, duties, rights, prophecies, warnings and challenges, are loaded in each day.

Do you know the language, command or decree you can use to claim what belongs to you in each day of the week? Do you know in Christendom, Monday can be equated to one of the days of creation in Genesis chapter one? Do you know creation lasted for six days and God rested on the seventh day? What day of the week can Christian equate as the first day of the week, if we follow Christian calendar? What day can we call day seven?

This book shall give insight to these questions. It shall explain how you can command each day of the week according to creation in the book of Genesis chapter one.

Above all, you shall exercise your right and claim what is hidden in each day of the week.
Check for this in **COMMAND THE DAY: DAILY PRAYER BOOK**

2. **PRAYER TO REMEMBER DREAMS**

A lot of people are passing through this spiritual epidemic on a daily basis. Their dream life is epileptic, having no ability to remember all dreams they dream, or sometimes forget everything entirely. This is nothing but spiritual havoc you need to erase from your spiritual record.
The answer to every form of spiritual blackout

caused by spiritual erasers is found in, **PRAYER TO REMEMBER DREAMS**

3. **100% CONFESSIONS AND PROPHECIES TO LOCATE HELPERS AND HELPERS TO LOCATE YOU**

This is a wonderful book on confessions and prophecies to locate helpers and helpers to locate you. It is a prayer book loaded with over two thousand (2,000) prayer points.

The book unravels how to locate unknown helpers, prayers to arrest mind of helpers and prayers for manifestation after encounter with helpers.

4. <u>ANOINTING FOR ELEVENTH HOUR HELP: HOPE AND HELP FOR YOUR TURBULENT TIMES</u>

This book tells much of what to do at injury hour called eleventh hour. When you read and use this book as prescribed fear shall vanish in your life when pursuing a project, career or contract.

5. <u>PRAYER TO LOCATE HELPERS AND HELPERS TO LOCATE YOU</u>

Our divine helper is God. He created us to be together and be of help to one another. In the midst of no help we lost out, ending our journey in the wilderness.

There are keys assign to open right doors of life. You need right key to locate your helpers. Enough is enough; of suffering in silence.

With this book, you shall locate your helpers while your helpers shall locate you.

6. <u>FIRE FOR FIRE PART ONE: (PRAYER BOOK BOOK 1)</u>

This prayer book is fast at answering spiritual problems. It is a bulldozer prayer book, full of prayers all through. It is highly recommended for night vigil. Testimonies are pouring in daily from users of this book across the world!

7. <u>PRAYER FOR FRUIT OF THE WOMB: EXPECTING MOTHERS</u>

This prayer book is children magnet. By faith and believe in God Almighty, as soon as you use this book open doors to child bearing shall be yours. Amen

8. <u>PRAYER FOR PREGNANT WOMEN: WITH ALL CHRISTIAN NAMES AND MEANINGS</u>

This is a spiritual prayer book loaded with prayers of solution for pregnant women. As soon as you take in, the prayers you shall pray from day one of conception to the day of delivery are written in this book.

9. <u>WARFARE IN THE OFFICE: PRAYER TO SILENCE TOUGH TIMES IN OFFICE</u>

It is high time you pray prayers of power must change hands in office. Use this book and liberate yourself from every form of office yoke.

10. <u>MY MARRIAGE SHALL NOT BREAK: THE SECRET TO LOVE AND MARRIAGE THAT LASTS</u>

Marriage is corner piece of life, happiness and joy. You need to hold it tight and guide it from wicked intruders and destroyer of homes.

11. <u>VICTORY OVER SATANIC HOUSE PART ONE: RIDDING YOUR HOME OF SPIRITUAL DARKNESS</u>

Are you a tenant, Land lord bombarded left and right, front and back by wicked people around you?
With this book you shall be liberated from the hooks of the enemy.

12. <u>DICTIONARY OF DREAMS: THE DREAM INTERPRETATION</u>

DICTIONARY WITH SYMBOLS, SIGNS, AND MEANINGS

This is a must book for every home. It gives accurate details to about **10,000 (Ten thousand) dreams and interpretations,** written in alphabetical order for quick reference and easy digestion. The book portrays spiritual revelations with sound prophetic guidelines. It is loaded with Biblical references and violent prayers.

Ask for yours today.

For Further Enquiries Contact
**THE AUTHOR
EVANGELIST TELLA OLAYERI
P.O. Box 1872 Shomolu Lagos.
Tel: 08023583168**

FROM AUTHOR'S DESK

BEFORE YOU GO

Hello,

Thank you for purchasing this book. Would you consider posting a review about this book? In addition to providing feedback and arousing others into Christ's bosom, reviews can help other customers to know about the book.

Please take a minute to leave a review on this book.

I would appreciate that!

Thank you in advance, for your review and your patronage!!

Feel free to drop us your prayer request. We will join faith with you and God's power will be released in your life and issue in question.

http://tellaolayeri.com/prayerrequest.php

NOTE: You can get all my books from my website **http://tellaolayeri.com**

GOOD NEWS!!!

My audiobook is now available, to get one visit **acx.com** and search **"Tella Olayeri."**

Brethren, to be loaded and reloaded visit: **amazon.com/author/tellaolayeri** for a full spiritual sojourn for my books.

Thanks.